This Planner Belongs To:

NAME: _____

CONTACT: _____

EMAIL: _____

INDEX

No.	Project	No.	Project
			Sewing Goals/Bucket List

SEWING PROJECT NO.

Date Started | Date Finished

Name: _____   **Personal**   **For:** _____

Pattern: _____   **Theme:** _____

Type: _____   **Final Cost:** _____

📏 MEASUREMENTS

🪡 SKETCH

🧵 MACHINE SETTINGS

✂️ MATERIALS/NOTIONS

_____

_____

_____

_____

_____

_____

_____

_____

🎨 COLOR SCHEME

✅ TO DO

_____

_____

_____

_____

_____

_____

_____

🎞️ FABRIC SWATCH | 🏠 USE FOR

IDEAS & NOTES
*Inspiration, Construction Notes/Details, In-Progress Notes, Alterations, Cost Breakdown, Etc.

RESULTS & FUTURE MAKES
*Post-Project Notes, New Techniques Learned, Care Instructions, Notes For Next Time, Etc.

SEWING PROJECT NO.

Name: **Personal**   **For:**

Pattern: **Theme:**

Type: **Final Cost:**

📏 MEASUREMENTS

🪡 MACHINE SETTINGS

🧷 MATERIALS/NOTIONS

_____

_____

_____

_____

_____

_____

_____

✔ TO DO

_____

_____

_____

_____

_____

_____

_____

👕 SKETCH

🎨 COLOR SCHEME

🪟 FABRIC SWATCH | 📐 USE FOR

IDEAS & NOTES
*Inspiration, Construction Notes/Details, In-Progress Notes, Alterations, Cost Breakdown, Etc.

RESULTS & FUTURE MAKES
*Post-Project Notes, New Techniques Learned, Care Instructions, Notes For Next Time, Etc.

SEWING PROJECT NO.

Name: Personal   **For:**

Pattern: **Theme:**

Type: **Final Cost:**

📏 MEASUREMENTS

🪡 MACHINE SETTINGS

✂ MATERIALS/NOTIONS

_____
_____
_____
_____
_____
_____
_____
_____

✓ TO DO

_____
_____
_____
_____
_____
_____
_____
_____

👕 SKETCH

🎨 COLOR SCHEME

▦ FABRIC SWATCH | 📐 USE FOR

IDEAS & NOTES
*Inspiration, Construction Notes/Details, In-Progress Notes, Alterations, Cost Breakdown, Etc.

RESULTS & FUTURE MAKES
*Post-Project Notes, New Techniques Learned, Care Instructions, Notes For Next Time, Etc.

SEWING PROJECT NO.

Date Started | Date Finished

Name: | Personal   For:
Pattern: | Theme:
Type: | Final Cost:

📏 MEASUREMENTS

🧵 MACHINE SETTINGS

✂ MATERIALS/NOTIONS

_____
_____
_____
_____
_____
_____
_____
_____

✔ TO DO

_____
_____
_____
_____
_____
_____
_____
_____
_____

👕 SKETCH

🎨 COLOR SCHEME

🔲 FABRIC SWATCH   👢 USE FOR

IDEAS & NOTES
*Inspiration, Construction Notes/Details, In-Progress Notes, Alterations, Cost Breakdown, Etc.

RESULTS & FUTURE MAKES
*Post-Project Notes, New Techniques Learned, Care Instructions, Notes For Next Time, Etc.

SEWING PROJECT NO.

Date Started | Date Finished

Name: _____ **Personal** **For:** _____
Pattern: _____ **Theme:** _____
Type: _____ **Final Cost:** _____

📏 MEASUREMENTS

👕 SKETCH

🧵 MACHINE SETTINGS

✂ MATERIALS/NOTIONS

- _____
- _____
- _____
- _____
- _____
- _____
- _____
- _____
- _____

🎨 COLOR SCHEME

✔ TO DO

- _____
- _____
- _____
- _____
- _____
- _____
- _____
- _____

🟦 FABRIC SWATCH | 👢 USE FOR

IDEAS & NOTES
*Inspiration, Construction Notes/Details, In-Progress Notes, Alterations, Cost Breakdown, Etc.

RESULTS & FUTURE MAKES
*Post-Project Notes, New Techniques Learned, Care Instructions, Notes For Next Time, Etc.

SEWING PROJECT NO.

Name: _____ Personal   **For:** _____

Pattern: _____ **Theme:** _____

Type: _____ **Final Cost:** _____

📏 MEASUREMENTS

🧵 SKETCH

🪡 MACHINE SETTINGS

✂️ MATERIALS/NOTIONS

- _____
- _____
- _____
- _____
- _____
- _____
- _____
- _____

🎨 COLOR SCHEME

✓ TO DO

- _____
- _____
- _____
- _____
- _____
- _____
- _____

▦ FABRIC SWATCH   ## 📐 USE FOR

IDEAS & NOTES
*Inspiration, Construction Notes/Details, In-Progress Notes, Alterations, Cost Breakdown, Etc.

RESULTS & FUTURE MAKES
*Post-Project Notes, New Techniques Learned, Care Instructions, Notes For Next Time, Etc.

SEWING PROJECT NO.

Date Started | Date Finished

Name: _____ **Personal** **For:** _____
Pattern: _____ **Theme:** _____
Type: _____ **Final Cost:** _____

📏 MEASUREMENTS

🪡 MACHINE SETTINGS

✂ MATERIALS/NOTIONS

- _____
- _____
- _____
- _____
- _____
- _____
- _____
- _____

✓ TO DO

- _____
- _____
- _____
- _____
- _____
- _____
- _____

👕 SKETCH

🎨 COLOR SCHEME

▦ FABRIC SWATCH   🏰 USE FOR

IDEAS & NOTES
*Inspiration, Construction Notes/Details, In-Progress Notes, Alterations, Cost Breakdown, Etc.

RESULTS & FUTURE MAKES
*Post-Project Notes, New Techniques Learned, Care Instructions, Notes For Next Time, Etc.

SEWING PROJECT NO.

Date Started | Date Finished

Name: _____ Personal **For:** _____

Pattern: _____ **Theme:** _____

Type: _____ **Final Cost:** _____

📏 MEASUREMENTS

🪡 MACHINE SETTINGS

✂ MATERIALS/NOTIONS

- _____
- _____
- _____
- _____
- _____
- _____
- _____
- _____
- _____

✔ TO DO

- _____
- _____
- _____
- _____
- _____
- _____
- _____
- _____

👕 SKETCH

🎨 COLOR SCHEME

▦ FABRIC SWATCH | 🏠 USE FOR

IDEAS & NOTES
*Inspiration, Construction Notes/Details, In-Progress Notes, Alterations, Cost Breakdown, Etc.

RESULTS & FUTURE MAKES
*Post-Project Notes, New Techniques Learned, Care Instructions, Notes For Next Time, Etc.

SEWING PROJECT NO.

Date Started | Date Finished

Name: Personal   For:

Pattern: Theme:

Type: Final Cost:

🧵 MEASUREMENTS

🪡 SKETCH

🖨 MACHINE SETTINGS

✂ MATERIALS/NOTIONS

_____

_____

_____

_____

_____

_____

_____

_____

✅ TO DO

_____

_____

_____

_____

_____

_____

_____

🎨 COLOR SCHEME

🗔 FABRIC SWATCH | 🏠 USE FOR

IDEAS & NOTES
*Inspiration, Construction Notes/Details, In-Progress Notes, Alterations, Cost Breakdown, Etc.

RESULTS & FUTURE MAKES
*Post-Project Notes, New Techniques Learned, Care Instructions, Notes For Next Time, Etc.

SEWING PROJECT NO.

Date Started | Date Finished

Name: | **Personal** | **For:**
Pattern: | **Theme:**
Type: | **Final Cost:**

📏 MEASUREMENTS

🪡 MACHINE SETTINGS

✂ MATERIALS/NOTIONS

_____
_____
_____
_____
_____
_____
_____
_____

✓ TO DO

_____
_____
_____
_____
_____
_____
_____
_____

👕 SKETCH

🎨 COLOR SCHEME

🏁 FABRIC SWATCH | 🏚 USE FOR

IDEAS & NOTES
*Inspiration, Construction Notes/Details, In-Progress Notes, Alterations, Cost Breakdown, Etc.

RESULTS & FUTURE MAKES
*Post-Project Notes, New Techniques Learned, Care Instructions, Notes For Next Time, Etc.

SEWING PROJECT NO.

| Date Started | Date Finished |

Name: **Personal**   **For:**

Pattern: **Theme:**

Type: **Final Cost:**

📏 MEASUREMENTS

🧵 MACHINE SETTINGS

✂ MATERIALS/NOTIONS

- _____
- _____
- _____
- _____
- _____
- _____
- _____
- _____
- _____

✓ TO DO

- _____
- _____
- _____
- _____
- _____
- _____
- _____
- _____

👕 SKETCH

🎨 COLOR SCHEME

▦ FABRIC SWATCH | 📐 USE FOR

IDEAS & NOTES
*Inspiration, Construction Notes/Details, In-Progress Notes, Alterations, Cost Breakdown, Etc.

RESULTS & FUTURE MAKES
*Post-Project Notes, New Techniques Learned, Care Instructions, Notes For Next Time, Etc.

SEWING PROJECT NO.

Name: Personal   For:

Pattern: Theme:

Type: Final Cost:

📏 MEASUREMENTS

🪡 MACHINE SETTINGS

✂ MATERIALS/NOTIONS

_____

_____

_____

_____

_____

_____

_____

_____

✓ TO DO

_____

_____

_____

_____

_____

_____

_____

👕 SKETCH

🎨 COLOR SCHEME

▦ FABRIC SWATCH   🏛 USE FOR

IDEAS & NOTES
*Inspiration, Construction Notes/Details, In-Progress Notes, Alterations, Cost Breakdown, Etc.

RESULTS & FUTURE MAKES
*Post-Project Notes, New Techniques Learned, Care Instructions, Notes For Next Time, Etc.

SEWING PROJECT NO.

Name: **Personal**   **For:**

Pattern: **Theme:**

Type: **Final Cost:**

📏 MEASUREMENTS

🪡 MACHINE SETTINGS

✂ MATERIALS/NOTIONS

- _____
- _____
- _____
- _____
- _____
- _____
- _____
- _____

✓ TO DO

- _____
- _____
- _____
- _____
- _____
- _____
- _____

👕 SKETCH

🎨 COLOR SCHEME

🪟 FABRIC SWATCH   🏷 USE FOR

IDEAS & NOTES
*Inspiration, Construction Notes/Details, In-Progress Notes, Alterations, Cost Breakdown, Etc.

RESULTS & FUTURE MAKES
*Post-Project Notes, New Techniques Learned, Care Instructions, Notes For Next Time, Etc.

SEWING PROJECT NO.

Date Started | Date Finished

Name: _____ Personal For: _____
Pattern: _____ Theme: _____
Type: _____ Final Cost: _____

📏 MEASUREMENTS

🪡 MACHINE SETTINGS

✂ MATERIALS/NOTIONS

- _____
- _____
- _____
- _____
- _____
- _____
- _____
- _____

✓ TO DO

- _____
- _____
- _____
- _____
- _____
- _____
- _____

👕 SKETCH

🎨 COLOR SCHEME

▦ FABRIC SWATCH | 🏠 USE FOR

IDEAS & NOTES
*Inspiration, Construction Notes/Details, In-Progress Notes, Alterations, Cost Breakdown, Etc.

RESULTS & FUTURE MAKES
*Post-Project Notes, New Techniques Learned, Care Instructions, Notes For Next Time, Etc.

SEWING PROJECT NO.

Name: _____ Personal   **For:** _____

Pattern: _____ **Theme:** _____

Type: _____ **Final Cost:** _____

📏 MEASUREMENTS

🪡 MACHINE SETTINGS

✂ MATERIALS/NOTIONS

- _____
- _____
- _____
- _____
- _____
- _____
- _____
- _____

✓ TO DO

- _____
- _____
- _____
- _____
- _____
- _____
- _____

👕 SKETCH

🎨 COLOR SCHEME

▦ FABRIC SWATCH   🏠 USE FOR

IDEAS & NOTES
*Inspiration, Construction Notes/Details, In-Progress Notes, Alterations, Cost Breakdown, Etc.

RESULTS & FUTURE MAKES
*Post-Project Notes, New Techniques Learned, Care Instructions, Notes For Next Time, Etc.

SEWING PROJECT NO.

Date Started | Date Finished

Name: | Personal | For:
Pattern: | Theme:
Type: | Final Cost:

📏 MEASUREMENTS

🪡 MACHINE SETTINGS

✂ MATERIALS/NOTIONS

_____
_____
_____
_____
_____
_____
_____
_____
_____

✓ TO DO

_____
_____
_____
_____
_____
_____
_____
_____
_____

👕 SKETCH

🎨 COLOR SCHEME

🧵 FABRIC SWATCH | 🏷 USE FOR

IDEAS & NOTES
*Inspiration, Construction Notes/Details, In-Progress Notes, Alterations, Cost Breakdown, Etc.

RESULTS & FUTURE MAKES
*Post-Project Notes, New Techniques Learned, Care Instructions, Notes For Next Time, Etc.

SEWING PROJECT NO.

Name: **Personal**   For:

Pattern: **Theme:**

Type: **Final Cost:**

📏 MEASUREMENTS

🪡 MACHINE SETTINGS

✂ MATERIALS/NOTIONS

- _____
- _____
- _____
- _____
- _____
- _____
- _____
- _____

✓ TO DO

- _____
- _____
- _____
- _____
- _____
- _____
- _____

👕 SKETCH

🎨 COLOR SCHEME

🏁 FABRIC SWATCH | 🏠 USE FOR

IDEAS & NOTES
*Inspiration, Construction Notes/Details, In-Progress Notes, Alterations, Cost Breakdown, Etc.

RESULTS & FUTURE MAKES
*Post-Project Notes, New Techniques Learned, Care Instructions, Notes For Next Time, Etc.

SEWING PROJECT NO.

Name: _____ **Personal** **For:** _____
Pattern: _____ **Theme:** _____
Type: _____ **Final Cost:** _____

📏 MEASUREMENTS

👕 SKETCH

🪡 MACHINE SETTINGS

✂ MATERIALS/NOTIONS

- _____
- _____
- _____
- _____
- _____
- _____
- _____
- _____

🎨 COLOR SCHEME

✓ TO DO

- _____
- _____
- _____
- _____
- _____
- _____
- _____

🧵 FABRIC SWATCH   👢 USE FOR

IDEAS & NOTES
*Inspiration, Construction Notes/Details, In-Progress Notes, Alterations, Cost Breakdown, Etc.

RESULTS & FUTURE MAKES
*Post-Project Notes, New Techniques Learned, Care Instructions, Notes For Next Time, Etc.

SEWING PROJECT NO.

Date Started | Date Finished

Name: Personal   For:
Pattern: Theme:
Type: Final Cost:

🧵 MEASUREMENTS

🪡 MACHINE SETTINGS

✂ MATERIALS/NOTIONS

_____
_____
_____
_____
_____
_____
_____
_____
_____

✓ TO DO

_____
_____
_____
_____
_____
_____
_____

👕 SKETCH

🎨 COLOR SCHEME

🗔 FABRIC SWATCH   🏠 USE FOR

IDEAS & NOTES
*Inspiration, Construction Notes/Details, In-Progress Notes, Alterations, Cost Breakdown, Etc.

RESULTS & FUTURE MAKES
*Post-Project Notes, New Techniques Learned, Care Instructions, Notes For Next Time, Etc.

SEWING PROJECT NO.

| Date Started | Date Finished |

Name:

Personal   For:

Pattern: Theme:

Type: Final Cost:

📏 MEASUREMENTS

👕 SKETCH

🪡 MACHINE SETTINGS

✂ MATERIALS/NOTIONS

_____
_____
_____
_____
_____
_____
_____
_____
_____

🎨 COLOR SCHEME

✓ TO DO

_____
_____
_____
_____
_____
_____
_____
_____

🧵 FABRIC SWATCH   🏠 USE FOR

IDEAS & NOTES
*Inspiration, Construction Notes/Details, In-Progress Notes, Alterations, Cost Breakdown, Etc.

RESULTS & FUTURE MAKES
*Post-Project Notes, New Techniques Learned, Care Instructions, Notes For Next Time, Etc.

SEWING PROJECT NO.

Date Started | Date Finished

Name: _____ Personal ___ For: _____
Pattern: _____ Theme: _____
Type: _____ Final Cost: _____

📏 MEASUREMENTS

🪡 SKETCH

🧵 MACHINE SETTINGS

✂️ MATERIALS/NOTIONS

- _____
- _____
- _____
- _____
- _____
- _____
- _____
- _____

🎨 COLOR SCHEME

🔲 FABRIC SWATCH | 📐 USE FOR

✓ TO DO

- _____
- _____
- _____
- _____
- _____
- _____
- _____
- _____

IDEAS & NOTES
*Inspiration, Construction Notes/Details, In-Progress Notes, Alterations, Cost Breakdown, Etc.

RESULTS & FUTURE MAKES
*Post-Project Notes, New Techniques Learned, Care Instructions, Notes For Next Time, Etc.

SEWING PROJECT NO.

Date Started | Date Finished

Name: Personal   For:

Pattern: Theme:

Type: Final Cost:

📏 MEASUREMENTS

🧵 SKETCH

🪡 MACHINE SETTINGS

✂ MATERIALS/NOTIONS

_____
_____
_____
_____
_____
_____
_____
_____
_____

🎨 COLOR SCHEME

✓ TO DO

_____
_____
_____
_____
_____
_____
_____

▦ FABRIC SWATCH   🏭 USE FOR

IDEAS & NOTES
*Inspiration, Construction Notes/Details, In-Progress Notes, Alterations, Cost Breakdown, Etc.

RESULTS & FUTURE MAKES
*Post-Project Notes, New Techniques Learned, Care Instructions, Notes For Next Time, Etc.

SEWING PROJECT NO.

Date Started | Date Finished

Name: Personal   For:

Pattern: Theme:

Type: Final Cost:

📏 MEASUREMENTS

🪡 MACHINE SETTINGS

✂ MATERIALS/NOTIONS

- _____
- _____
- _____
- _____
- _____
- _____
- _____
- _____
- _____

✓ TO DO

- _____
- _____
- _____
- _____
- _____
- _____
- _____
- _____

👕 SKETCH

🎨 COLOR SCHEME

▦ FABRIC SWATCH   🏛 USE FOR

IDEAS & NOTES
*Inspiration, Construction Notes/Details, In-Progress Notes, Alterations, Cost Breakdown, Etc.

RESULTS & FUTURE MAKES
*Post-Project Notes, New Techniques Learned, Care Instructions, Notes For Next Time, Etc.

SEWING PROJECT NO.

Date Started | Date Finished

Name: **Personal**   **For:**

Pattern: **Theme:**

Type: **Final Cost:**

MEASUREMENTS

MACHINE SETTINGS

MATERIALS/NOTIONS

_____
_____
_____
_____
_____
_____
_____
_____

TO DO

_____
_____
_____
_____
_____
_____
_____
_____

SKETCH

COLOR SCHEME

FABRIC SWATCH   USE FOR

IDEAS & NOTES
*Inspiration, Construction Notes/Details, In-Progress Notes, Alterations, Cost Breakdown, Etc.

RESULTS & FUTURE MAKES
*Post-Project Notes, New Techniques Learned, Care Instructions, Notes For Next Time, Etc.

SEWING PROJECT NO.

Date Started | Date Finished

Name: _____ Personal   For: _____
Pattern: _____ Theme: _____
Type: _____ Final Cost: _____

📏 MEASUREMENTS

🪡 MACHINE SETTINGS

✂ MATERIALS/NOTIONS

- _____
- _____
- _____
- _____
- _____
- _____
- _____
- _____

✓ TO DO

- _____
- _____
- _____
- _____
- _____
- _____
- _____

👕 SKETCH

🎨 COLOR SCHEME

FABRIC SWATCH | 👢 USE FOR

IDEAS & NOTES
*Inspiration, Construction Notes/Details, In-Progress Notes, Alterations, Cost Breakdown, Etc.

RESULTS & FUTURE MAKES
*Post-Project Notes, New Techniques Learned, Care Instructions, Notes For Next Time, Etc.

SEWING PROJECT NO.

Date Started | Date Finished

Name: **Personal**   **For:**

Pattern: **Theme:**

Type: **Final Cost:**

📏 MEASUREMENTS

🪡 MACHINE SETTINGS

✂ MATERIALS/NOTIONS

_____

_____

_____

_____

_____

_____

_____

_____

✓ TO DO

_____

_____

_____

_____

_____

_____

👕 SKETCH

🎨 COLOR SCHEME

▦ FABRIC SWATCH | 🏠 USE FOR

IDEAS & NOTES
*Inspiration, Construction Notes/Details, In-Progress Notes, Alterations, Cost Breakdown, Etc.

RESULTS & FUTURE MAKES
*Post-Project Notes, New Techniques Learned, Care Instructions, Notes For Next Time, Etc.

SEWING PROJECT NO.

Name: _____ Personal For: _____

Pattern: _____ **Theme:** _____

Type: _____ **Final Cost:** _____

📏 MEASUREMENTS

🪡 SKETCH

🧵 MACHINE SETTINGS

✂ MATERIALS/NOTIONS

- _____
- _____
- _____
- _____
- _____
- _____
- _____
- _____
- _____

🎨 COLOR SCHEME

✓ TO DO

- _____
- _____
- _____
- _____
- _____
- _____
- _____
- _____
- _____

🏚 FABRIC SWATCH   📐 USE FOR

IDEAS & NOTES
*Inspiration, Construction Notes/Details, In-Progress Notes, Alterations, Cost Breakdown, Etc.

RESULTS & FUTURE MAKES
*Post-Project Notes, New Techniques Learned, Care Instructions, Notes For Next Time, Etc.

SEWING PROJECT NO.

Date Started | Date Finished

Name: | Personal | For:
Pattern: | Theme:
Type: | Final Cost:

📏 MEASUREMENTS

👕 SKETCH

🪡 MACHINE SETTINGS

✂ MATERIALS/NOTIONS

_____
_____
_____
_____
_____
_____
_____
_____

🎨 COLOR SCHEME

✓ TO DO

_____
_____
_____
_____
_____
_____
_____

🧵 FABRIC SWATCH | 📐 USE FOR

IDEAS & NOTES
*Inspiration, Construction Notes/Details, In-Progress Notes, Alterations, Cost Breakdown, Etc.

RESULTS & FUTURE MAKES
*Post-Project Notes, New Techniques Learned, Care Instructions, Notes For Next Time, Etc.

SEWING PROJECT NO.

Name: _____ **Personal** **For:** _____
Pattern: _____ **Theme:** _____
Type: _____ **Final Cost:** _____

📏 MEASUREMENTS

🪡 MACHINE SETTINGS

✂ MATERIALS/NOTIONS

- _____
- _____
- _____
- _____
- _____
- _____
- _____
- _____
- _____

✓ TO DO

- _____
- _____
- _____
- _____
- _____
- _____
- _____
- _____

👕 SKETCH

🎨 COLOR SCHEME

▦ FABRIC SWATCH   📐 USE FOR

IDEAS & NOTES
*Inspiration, Construction Notes/Details, In-Progress Notes, Alterations, Cost Breakdown, Etc.

RESULTS & FUTURE MAKES
*Post-Project Notes, New Techniques Learned, Care Instructions, Notes For Next Time, Etc.

SEWING PROJECT NO.

Name: **Personal**   **For:**

Pattern: **Theme:**

Type: **Final Cost:**

📏 MEASUREMENTS

👕 SKETCH

🪡 MACHINE SETTINGS

✂ MATERIALS/NOTIONS

- _____
- _____
- _____
- _____
- _____
- _____
- _____
- _____
- _____

🎨 COLOR SCHEME

✔ TO DO

- _____
- _____
- _____
- _____
- _____
- _____
- _____
- _____
- _____

▦ FABRIC SWATCH   USE FOR

IDEAS & NOTES
*Inspiration, Construction Notes/Details, In-Progress Notes, Alterations, Cost Breakdown, Etc.

RESULTS & FUTURE MAKES
*Post-Project Notes, New Techniques Learned, Care Instructions, Notes For Next Time, Etc.

SEWING PROJECT NO.

Name: **Personal** **For:**
Pattern: **Theme:**
Type: **Final Cost:**

📏 MEASUREMENTS

👕 SKETCH

🧵 MACHINE SETTINGS

✂ MATERIALS/NOTIONS

_____
_____
_____
_____
_____
_____
_____
_____
_____

🎨 COLOR SCHEME

✅ TO DO

_____
_____
_____
_____
_____
_____
_____

🏁 FABRIC SWATCH   🏗 USE FOR

IDEAS & NOTES
*Inspiration, Construction Notes/Details, In-Progress Notes, Alterations, Cost Breakdown, Etc.

RESULTS & FUTURE MAKES
*Post-Project Notes, New Techniques Learned, Care Instructions, Notes For Next Time, Etc.

SEWING PROJECT NO.

Name: **Personal**   **For:**

Pattern: **Theme:**

Type: **Final Cost:**

📏 MEASUREMENTS

🪡 MACHINE SETTINGS

✂ MATERIALS/NOTIONS

- _____
- _____
- _____
- _____
- _____
- _____
- _____
- _____
- _____

✏ TO DO

- _____
- _____
- _____
- _____
- _____
- _____
- _____

👕 SKETCH

🎨 COLOR SCHEME

🪡 FABRIC SWATCH   📐 USE FOR

IDEAS & NOTES
*Inspiration, Construction Notes/Details, In-Progress Notes, Alterations, Cost Breakdown, Etc.

RESULTS & FUTURE MAKES
*Post-Project Notes, New Techniques Learned, Care Instructions, Notes For Next Time, Etc.

SEWING PROJECT NO.

Name: **Personal**   **For:**

Pattern: **Theme:**

Type: **Final Cost:**

🧵 MEASUREMENTS

🪡 MACHINE SETTINGS

✂ MATERIALS/NOTIONS

_____
_____
_____
_____
_____
_____
_____

✓ TO DO

_____
_____
_____
_____
_____
_____
_____

👕 SKETCH

🎨 COLOR SCHEME

▦ FABRIC SWATCH   🏠 USE FOR

IDEAS & NOTES
*Inspiration, Construction Notes/Details, In-Progress Notes, Alterations, Cost Breakdown, Etc.

RESULTS & FUTURE MAKES
*Post-Project Notes, New Techniques Learned, Care Instructions, Notes For Next Time, Etc.

SEWING PROJECT NO.

Date Started | Date Finished

Name: **Personal**   **For:**

Pattern: **Theme:**

Type: **Final Cost:**

📏 MEASUREMENTS

🪡 MACHINE SETTINGS

✂ MATERIALS/NOTIONS

_____
_____
_____
_____
_____
_____
_____

✓ TO DO

_____
_____
_____
_____
_____
_____
_____
_____

👕 SKETCH

🎨 COLOR SCHEME

▦ FABRIC SWATCH   📐 USE FOR

IDEAS & NOTES
*Inspiration, Construction Notes/Details, In-Progress Notes, Alterations, Cost Breakdown, Etc.

RESULTS & FUTURE MAKES
*Post-Project Notes, New Techniques Learned, Care Instructions, Notes For Next Time, Etc.

SEWING PROJECT NO.

Name: **Personal**   **For:**

Pattern: **Theme:**

Type: **Final Cost:**

📏 MEASUREMENTS

🧵 MACHINE SETTINGS

✂ MATERIALS/NOTIONS

_____
_____
_____
_____
_____
_____
_____
_____

✅ TO DO

_____
_____
_____
_____
_____
_____
_____

👕 SKETCH

🎨 COLOR SCHEME

🖼 FABRIC SWATCH   📐 USE FOR

IDEAS & NOTES
*Inspiration, Construction Notes/Details, In-Progress Notes, Alterations, Cost Breakdown, Etc.

RESULTS & FUTURE MAKES
*Post-Project Notes, New Techniques Learned, Care Instructions, Notes For Next Time, Etc.

SEWING PROJECT NO.

Name: _____ Personal   For:

Pattern: Theme:

Type: Final Cost:

🧵 MEASUREMENTS

🪡 MACHINE SETTINGS

✂ MATERIALS/NOTIONS

_____
_____
_____
_____
_____
_____
_____
_____
_____

✓ TO DO

_____
_____
_____
_____
_____
_____
_____
_____

👕 SKETCH

🎨 COLOR SCHEME

🏷 FABRIC SWATCH   🏠 USE FOR

IDEAS & NOTES
*Inspiration, Construction Notes/Details, In-Progress Notes, Alterations, Cost Breakdown, Etc.

RESULTS & FUTURE MAKES
*Post-Project Notes, New Techniques Learned, Care Instructions, Notes For Next Time, Etc.

SEWING PROJECT NO.

| Date Started | Date Finished |

Name: **Personal**   **For:**

Pattern: **Theme:**

Type: **Final Cost:**

📏 MEASUREMENTS

🪡 MACHINE SETTINGS

✂ MATERIALS/NOTIONS

- _____
- _____
- _____
- _____
- _____
- _____
- _____
- _____

✓ TO DO

- _____
- _____
- _____
- _____
- _____
- _____
- _____

👕 SKETCH

🎨 COLOR SCHEME

🖼 FABRIC SWATCH   📐 USE FOR

IDEAS & NOTES
*Inspiration, Construction Notes/Details, In-Progress Notes, Alterations, Cost Breakdown, Etc.

RESULTS & FUTURE MAKES
*Post-Project Notes, New Techniques Learned, Care Instructions, Notes For Next Time, Etc.

SEWING PROJECT NO.

Name: Personal   **For:**

Pattern: **Theme:**

Type: **Final Cost:**

🧵 MEASUREMENTS

🧵 MACHINE SETTINGS

✂ MATERIALS/NOTIONS

✓ TO DO

👕 SKETCH

🎨 COLOR SCHEME

▦ FABRIC SWATCH   🏠 USE FOR

IDEAS & NOTES
*Inspiration, Construction Notes/Details, In-Progress Notes, Alterations, Cost Breakdown, Etc.

RESULTS & FUTURE MAKES
*Post-Project Notes, New Techniques Learned, Care Instructions, Notes For Next Time, Etc.

SEWING PROJECT NO.

Date Started | Date Finished

Name: _____ Personal For: _____
Pattern: _____ Theme: _____
Type: _____ Final Cost: _____

📏 MEASUREMENTS

🧵 MACHINE SETTINGS

✂ MATERIALS/NOTIONS

- _____
- _____
- _____
- _____
- _____
- _____
- _____
- _____
- _____

✓ TO DO

- _____
- _____
- _____
- _____
- _____
- _____
- _____
- _____

👕 SKETCH

🎨 COLOR SCHEME

🖼 FABRIC SWATCH | 🏷 USE FOR

IDEAS & NOTES
*Inspiration, Construction Notes/Details, In-Progress Notes, Alterations, Cost Breakdown, Etc.

RESULTS & FUTURE MAKES
*Post-Project Notes, New Techniques Learned, Care Instructions, Notes For Next Time, Etc.

SEWING PROJECT NO.

Date Started | Date Finished

Name: | **Personal** **For:**
Pattern: | **Theme:**
Type: | **Final Cost:**

📏 MEASUREMENTS

🧵 MACHINE SETTINGS

✂ MATERIALS/NOTIONS

- _____
- _____
- _____
- _____
- _____
- _____
- _____

✓ TO DO

- _____
- _____
- _____
- _____
- _____
- _____

👕 SKETCH

🎨 COLOR SCHEME

▦ FABRIC SWATCH | 📐 USE FOR

IDEAS & NOTES
*Inspiration, Construction Notes/Details, In-Progress Notes, Alterations, Cost Breakdown, Etc.

RESULTS & FUTURE MAKES
*Post-Project Notes, New Techniques Learned, Care Instructions, Notes For Next Time, Etc.

SEWING PROJECT NO.

Date Started | Date Finished

Name: Personal   For:
Pattern: Theme:
Type: Final Cost:

📏 MEASUREMENTS

🪡 MACHINE SETTINGS

✂ MATERIALS/NOTIONS

- _____
- _____
- _____
- _____
- _____
- _____
- _____
- _____
- _____

✓ TO DO

- _____
- _____
- _____
- _____
- _____
- _____
- _____
- _____

👕 SKETCH

🎨 COLOR SCHEME

▦ FABRIC SWATCH | 🏠 USE FOR

IDEAS & NOTES
*Inspiration, Construction Notes/Details, In-Progress Notes, Alterations, Cost Breakdown, Etc.

RESULTS & FUTURE MAKES
*Post-Project Notes, New Techniques Learned, Care Instructions, Notes For Next Time, Etc.

SEWING PROJECT NO.

Date Started | Date Finished

Name: Personal   For:
Pattern: **Theme:**
Type: **Final Cost:**

🧵 MEASUREMENTS

🪡 MACHINE SETTINGS

✂ MATERIALS/NOTIONS

_____
_____
_____
_____
_____
_____
_____
_____
_____

✒ TO DO

_____
_____
_____
_____
_____
_____
_____
_____
_____

👕 SKETCH

🎨 COLOR SCHEME

▦ FABRIC SWATCH   📐 USE FOR

IDEAS & NOTES
*Inspiration, Construction Notes/Details, In-Progress Notes, Alterations, Cost Breakdown, Etc.

RESULTS & FUTURE MAKES
*Post-Project Notes, New Techniques Learned, Care Instructions, Notes For Next Time, Etc.

SEWING PROJECT NO.

Name: _____   **Personal**   **For:** _____
Pattern: _____   **Theme:** _____
Type: _____   **Final Cost:** _____

📏 MEASUREMENTS

👕 SKETCH

🪡 MACHINE SETTINGS

✂️ MATERIALS/NOTIONS

- _____
- _____
- _____
- _____
- _____
- _____
- _____
- _____

✓ TO DO

- _____
- _____
- _____
- _____
- _____
- _____
- _____

🎨 COLOR SCHEME

🔳 FABRIC SWATCH   📐 USE FOR

IDEAS & NOTES
*Inspiration, Construction Notes/Details, In-Progress Notes, Alterations, Cost Breakdown, Etc.

RESULTS & FUTURE MAKES
*Post-Project Notes, New Techniques Learned, Care Instructions, Notes For Next Time, Etc.

SEWING PROJECT NO.

Date Started | Date Finished

Name: **Personal**   **For:**
Pattern: **Theme:**
Type: **Final Cost:**

📏 MEASUREMENTS

👕 SKETCH

🧵 MACHINE SETTINGS

✂ MATERIALS/NOTIONS

- _____
- _____
- _____
- _____
- _____
- _____
- _____
- _____

🎨 COLOR SCHEME

✏ TO DO

- _____
- _____
- _____
- _____
- _____
- _____
- _____

🏁 FABRIC SWATCH   📐 USE FOR

IDEAS & NOTES
*Inspiration, Construction Notes/Details, In-Progress Notes, Alterations, Cost Breakdown, Etc.

RESULTS & FUTURE MAKES
*Post-Project Notes, New Techniques Learned, Care Instructions, Notes For Next Time, Etc.

SEWING PROJECT NO.

Name: Personal   For:

Pattern: Theme:

Type: Final Cost:

📏 MEASUREMENTS

🧵 MACHINE SETTINGS

✂ MATERIALS/NOTIONS

_____

_____

_____

_____

_____

_____

_____

_____

✓ TO DO

_____

_____

_____

_____

_____

_____

_____

_____

👕 SKETCH

🎨 COLOR SCHEME

🧵 FABRIC SWATCH   👜 USE FOR

IDEAS & NOTES
*Inspiration, Construction Notes/Details, In-Progress Notes, Alterations, Cost Breakdown, Etc.

RESULTS & FUTURE MAKES
*Post-Project Notes, New Techniques Learned, Care Instructions, Notes For Next Time, Etc.

SEWING PROJECT NO.

| Date Started | Date Finished |

Name:
Pattern:
Type:

Personal **For:**
Theme:
Final Cost:

📏 MEASUREMENTS

🪡 MACHINE SETTINGS

✂️ MATERIALS/NOTIONS

_____
_____
_____
_____
_____
_____
_____

✓ TO DO

_____
_____
_____
_____
_____
_____

👕 SKETCH

🎨 COLOR SCHEME

▦ FABRIC SWATCH · 📐 USE FOR

IDEAS & NOTES
*Inspiration, Construction Notes/Details, In-Progress Notes, Alterations, Cost Breakdown, Etc.

RESULTS & FUTURE MAKES
*Post-Project Notes, New Techniques Learned, Care Instructions, Notes For Next Time, Etc.

SEWING PROJECT NO.

Name: _____
Personal   For: _____

Pattern: _____
Theme: _____

Type: _____
Final Cost: _____

📏 MEASUREMENTS

👕 SKETCH

🪡 MACHINE SETTINGS

✂ MATERIALS/NOTIONS

_____

_____

_____

_____

_____

_____

_____

_____

_____

🎨 COLOR SCHEME

▦ FABRIC SWATCH   🏠 USE FOR

✅ TO DO

_____

_____

_____

_____

_____

_____

_____

_____

IDEAS & NOTES
*Inspiration, Construction Notes/Details, In-Progress Notes, Alterations, Cost Breakdown, Etc.

RESULTS & FUTURE MAKES
*Post-Project Notes, New Techniques Learned, Care Instructions, Notes For Next Time, Etc.

SEWING PROJECT NO.

Name: Personal   For:

Pattern: Theme:

Type: Final Cost:

📏 MEASUREMENTS

🪡 MACHINE SETTINGS

✂ MATERIALS/NOTIONS

- _____
- _____
- _____
- _____
- _____
- _____
- _____
- _____
- _____

✓ TO DO

- _____
- _____
- _____
- _____
- _____
- _____
- _____

👕 SKETCH

🎨 COLOR SCHEME

🪟 FABRIC SWATCH | 📐 USE FOR

IDEAS & NOTES
*Inspiration, Construction Notes/Details, In-Progress Notes, Alterations, Cost Breakdown, Etc.

RESULTS & FUTURE MAKES
*Post-Project Notes, New Techniques Learned, Care Instructions, Notes For Next Time, Etc.

SEWING PROJECT NO.

Date Started | Date Finished

Name: _____ Personal   For: _____
Pattern: _____ Theme: _____
Type: _____ Final Cost: _____

📏 MEASUREMENTS

👕 SKETCH

🖥 MACHINE SETTINGS

✂ MATERIALS/NOTIONS

_____
_____
_____
_____
_____
_____
_____
_____

🎨 COLOR SCHEME

✓ TO DO

_____
_____
_____
_____
_____
_____

🏢 FABRIC SWATCH   🏠 USE FOR

IDEAS & NOTES
*Inspiration, Construction Notes/Details, In-Progress Notes, Alterations, Cost Breakdown, Etc.

RESULTS & FUTURE MAKES
*Post-Project Notes, New Techniques Learned, Care Instructions, Notes For Next Time, Etc.

SEWING PROJECT NO.

Name: **Personal** **For:**

Pattern: **Theme:**

Type: **Final Cost:**

📏 MEASUREMENTS

🧵 MACHINE SETTINGS

🪡 MATERIALS/NOTIONS

- _____
- _____
- _____
- _____
- _____
- _____
- _____
- _____

✓ TO DO

- _____
- _____
- _____
- _____
- _____
- _____
- _____
- _____

👕 SKETCH

🎨 COLOR SCHEME

▦ FABRIC SWATCH | 📐 USE FOR

IDEAS & NOTES
*Inspiration, Construction Notes/Details, In-Progress Notes, Alterations, Cost Breakdown, Etc.

RESULTS & FUTURE MAKES
*Post-Project Notes, New Techniques Learned, Care Instructions, Notes For Next Time, Etc.

SEWING PROJECT NO.

Name: _____ Personal   For: _____

Pattern: _____ Theme: _____

Type: _____ Final Cost: _____

📏 MEASUREMENTS

👕 SKETCH

🪡 MACHINE SETTINGS

✂️ MATERIALS/NOTIONS

- _____
- _____
- _____
- _____
- _____
- _____
- _____
- _____

🎨 COLOR SCHEME

✔️ TO DO

- _____
- _____
- _____
- _____
- _____
- _____
- _____

🧵 FABRIC SWATCH   📐 USE FOR

IDEAS & NOTES
*Inspiration, Construction Notes/Details, In-Progress Notes, Alterations, Cost Breakdown, Etc.

RESULTS & FUTURE MAKES
*Post-Project Notes, New Techniques Learned, Care Instructions, Notes For Next Time, Etc.

SEWING PROJECT NO.

Date Started | Date Finished

Personal **For:**

Name:
Pattern:
Type:

Theme:
Final Cost:

📏 MEASUREMENTS

👕 SKETCH

🧵 MACHINE SETTINGS

✂ MATERIALS/NOTIONS

_____
_____
_____
_____
_____
_____
_____
_____

🎨 COLOR SCHEME

🪡 FABRIC SWATCH | 📐 USE FOR

✅ TO DO

_____
_____
_____
_____
_____
_____
_____
_____
_____

IDEAS & NOTES
*Inspiration, Construction Notes/Details, In-Progress Notes, Alterations, Cost Breakdown, Etc.

RESULTS & FUTURE MAKES
*Post-Project Notes, New Techniques Learned, Care Instructions, Notes For Next Time, Etc.

SEWING PROJECT NO.

Date Started | Date Finished

Name: | Personal | For:
Pattern: | Theme:
Type: | Final Cost:

📏 MEASUREMENTS

🪡 MACHINE SETTINGS

✂️ MATERIALS/NOTIONS

- _____
- _____
- _____
- _____
- _____
- _____
- _____
- _____
- _____

✏️ TO DO

- _____
- _____
- _____
- _____
- _____
- _____
- _____
- _____

👕 SKETCH

🎨 COLOR SCHEME

🏳️ FABRIC SWATCH | 📐 USE FOR

IDEAS & NOTES
*Inspiration, Construction Notes/Details, In-Progress Notes, Alterations, Cost Breakdown, Etc.

RESULTS & FUTURE MAKES
*Post-Project Notes, New Techniques Learned, Care Instructions, Notes For Next Time, Etc.

SEWING GOALS/BUCKET LIST

1		26	
2		27	
3		28	
4		29	
5		30	
6		31	
7		32	
8		33	
9		34	
10		35	
11		36	
12		37	
13		38	
14		39	
15		40	
16		41	
17		42	
18		43	
19		44	
20		45	
21		46	
22		47	
23		48	
24		49	
25		50	

Printed in Great Britain
by Amazon

35028297R00066